Transitioning Lives

By

Ricardo Fisher

Transitioning Lives

Preface

After finishing my first book, I was certain that the rest of my current lifetime was going to be Happiness, prosperity, inner peace, fulfilment, health and that the biggest obstacles in life were already a thing of the past. However, once again life surprised me with a challenge even greater than those experienced before.

About seven months ago, I was diagnosed with an illness that has put me in the hospital several times and the doctors have mentioned that my life expectancy is very slim, making me realized that my current lifetime in this earth is about to finish. Immediately the questions that arise are: Why is this happening to me? Is it the consequence of a Karma that I still have to pay? What is the purpose of this new challenge?

The value that this book aims to expose to readers is that what we have learned and continue to learn every day, are stages towards a true evolution where the final goal is to meet the Creator of the Universe and become One. But it is to be expected that, to reach that level, we must overcome many obstacles, tests, as well as satisfactory experiences and total fulfillment.

Transitioning Lives

Table of Contents

Transitioning Lives

Introduction

Did you know that before you were born you had already chosen your parents, your challenges and even your soul mate? I would like to introduce this fascinating concept that going through this spiritual process that occurs before and after death, the souls plan their next incarnation. Discover how the soul carefully selects the perfect people and circumstances for its evolution, guided by spiritual advice and full of wisdom. We will explore deep questions such as: How does a spirit choose its next parents? What role do karma and life lessons play in these decisions? What does it really mean to find your soulmate?

In addition, we explain how your gifts and challenges were planned to help you grow spiritually and fulfill your purpose in this life. This book is a window into the mysteries of spiritual planning, designed to inspire you and change the way you view your existence. Featured Topics: Choosing the soul before birth, the role of spirit guides in planning your life, connecting with soulmates and predestined relationships.

Chapter 1: What Society Teach Us

Stereotypes are generalized ideas and assumptions about the characteristics of specific groups of people, shaped by longstanding social and cultural beliefs. When it comes to children, these stereotypes often manifest as expectations that are implanted by family members, societal structures, educational systems, and the broader environment. These expectations dictate who they should become, what values they must uphold, and the life milestones they should aspire to such as completing their education, securing a stable and well-paid job, getting married, and having children. These socially constructed ideals are introduced subtly, but they embed themselves so deeply in a child's psyche that they eventually become perceived as absolute truths indisputable, fixed beliefs that define what it means to live a successful and happy life.

Over time, such beliefs are internalized to the extent that fulfillment, peace, and happiness are thought to be derived solely from external achievements. However, the deeper truth is often the opposite: joy, love, serenity, and success are fundamentally internal experiences. They originate within and do not require validation from material conditions or societal approval. Admittedly, this is far easier to say than to truly believe or implement it, especially in a world dominated by media narratives, digital influence, and peer pressure. Social platforms and advertising constantly bombard young people with glamorized symbols of "success" expensive cars, designer clothes, exotic vacations, real estate investments, and prestigious degrees suggesting that these are the benchmarks for a meaningful life.

Children, from their earliest developmental stages, are imprinted with generalized perceptions of how they are supposed to look, think, behave, or feel. These perceptions are based on societal ideals rather than individual truth. The beliefs are typically passed down through generations, rooted in cultural, religious, or institutional frameworks that may not always reflect the complexities of real life. Unfortunately, they are often accepted unquestioningly. Yet, real life is far more nuanced. The world is not black-and-white, and neither are the paths we take toward understanding ourselves.

It is essential to highlight that childhood is not just a phase of growth; it is the foundational stage where emotional, intellectual, and physical capacities begin to take form. The way a child is shaped during this phase will influence their patterns of thought, their behavior, and their emotional responses for the years to come unless disrupted by transformative experiences that force them to reconsider the assumptions they've long carried. These are what I refer to as "catalysts." They are pivotal moments of personal or spiritual upheaval that make us stop and question everything we once took for granted.

We often hear that childhood is the key to understanding why we are the way we are, and why we react in specific ways to life's challenges. This idea is not simply metaphorical; it is deeply rooted in psychology and human development. Many of us carry invisible wounds or traumas from early life some we are aware of, and some buried so deep that they influence us without our conscious knowledge. These unresolved experiences define our current perceptions, fears, strengths, and coping mechanisms. To move forward with clarity and intention, it becomes necessary to look back and understand the programming we received.

Think of it as a computing algorithm. When a developer codes a computer, they use specific paradigms and frameworks to instruct the system on how to respond to particular inputs. Similarly, society, family, media, religion, and peer groups all serve as programmers that create internal codes for how we behave, perceive, and react. These codes shape our identities and guide our choices. But sometimes, through crises or breakdowns, life gives us a chance to rewrite that code to evolve beyond it and align with our true, higher self.

As we've explored so far, our self-concept and behavioral patterns are largely inherited and reinforced over time. However, societal views on childhood have gradually evolved. Once, childhood was regarded merely as a preparatory stage for adulthood, with little understanding of its emotional and psychological depth. Over time, we transitioned toward recognizing the "best interests of the child" in decision-making. But even then, the concept was often vague or subjectively defined based either on a parent's beliefs or on socially accepted norms.

Today, we are beginning to embrace a more progressive model: one that sees children as autonomous individuals with voices, perspectives, and rights. They are increasingly recognized as agents who can influence their environment and contribute meaningfully to social dialogue. Yet despite this shift, societal expectations especially around success continue to exert a powerful, often subconscious influence on the choice's children make. Even when we give children the right to express themselves, their voices are filtered through an inherited lens of "what success should look like."

Society's standards for success are collective beliefs that establish what a "worthy" life should entail. These standards are projected onto children and continue into adulthood, creating immense pressure to conform. From a young age, we are taught to seek validation through academic achievement, financial security, social status, and outward appearances. These standards become so normalized that deviating from them feels like failure. Worse still, they shape how we judge not only ourselves but others around us.

As these expectations accumulate, they generate stress, confusion, and a disconnect from one's authentic self. However, life inevitably presents us with challenges that disrupt these illusions such as personal losses, illnesses, failures, or spiritual crises. These difficult experiences are not punishments; they are opportunities to reassess what truly matters. Such moments force us to move away from imitation, to stop living on autopilot, and to begin living with intention. They invite us to evaluate our values, appreciate our efforts, and recognize the subtle, powerful sources of light and love in our lives.

When we reflect in the midst of hardship, we may discover that what sustains us isn't wealth or status, but something much deeper: our connection to God, the comfort of family, the loyalty of true friends, and the unconditional love that cannot be bought or measured. These are the things that renew our strength, help us to rise again, and enable us to pursue genuine peace, joy, and personal fulfilment, the very things we deserve and long for.

It's easy to offer advice or write words of hope, but until one experiences the storm firsthand, the words remain abstract. Let me offer a simple yet powerful example: imagine a person lying in a hospital bed, unable to drive the luxury car they recently bought, or sleep in the grand mansion they own. If stepping outside that hospital means risking their life, do those possessions hold any real value in that moment? What truly matters then?

In the coming chapters, I will share several deeply personal moments episodes that shaped my journey and prompted me to start writing. At first, this writing was a private reflection, a therapeutic process to help me better understand myself. But eventually, it became a means to reach out to others. My hope is that these stories will resonate with readers navigating their own struggles and encourage them to find strength, meaning, and healing in their unique path forward.

Chapter 2: Traumatic Events for Evolution

Definition

A crisis can be defined as an unexpected, impactful, and transformative event that disrupts our status quo and significantly alters our perception of life. Such events not only affect us personally but also influence our environment and the people around us. These experiences often trigger intense emotional and psychological responses, including feelings of loneliness, desperation, anxiety, fear, and uncertainty.

Crises are typically classified in terms of severity, major or minor, but regardless of the categorization, their impact is real and deeply felt. Traumatic events, whether sudden or cumulative, can cause significant psychological distress. Examples include natural disasters, violent incidents, serious accidents, bereavement, medical emergencies, abuse, and various forms of personal loss. Each individual may experience and process these events differently, but their capacity to shake our emotional foundation is universal.

Recognizing the Signs That You May Be Going Through a Crisis

The experience of a personal crisis often manifests through emotional, cognitive, and behavioral changes. Below are some common indicators that may suggest an individual is undergoing a significant internal crisis:

- **A persistent sense of emptiness or a lack of purpose in life:** You may feel emotionally hollow, disconnected from your passions, or unsure of why you do what you do. These sensations are often accompanied by an internal questioning of your direction and meaning.

- **Increased self-questioning and reflection:** You might begin to revisit past or current life events with deep inquiry, asking questions such as: *Why did this happen to me? Why does this not happen to those who (in my opinion) deserve such outcomes?* This kind of existential questioning often signals the onset of internal transformation.

- **Experiencing anxiety and depression:** These emotional states become particularly intense when faced with uncertainty about the future, or when one feels powerless over how events will unfold. Feelings of dread, hopelessness, and the inability to see a clear path forward are common.

- **Loss of personal identity due to behavioral adaptation:** You may notice that you're frequently altering your thoughts, actions, or personality to meet others' expectations especially within close relationships such as marriage, parent-child dynamics, or among siblings. Over time, this can result in a deep disconnection from your authentic self.

- **Withdrawal and social isolation:** A person in crisis may begin to avoid friends, family, or social activities, preferring solitude even when it leads to further emotional decline. This withdrawal can paradoxically feel more comfortable than facing the external world.

- **Demotivation or lack of interest in life:** You might feel as though you've lost the drive to engage in daily routines, pursue your goals, or even envision a meaningful future. Life begins to feel stagnant, with no clear direction or ambition.

Chapter 3: How to Find the Purpose in The Middle of a Crisis?

Life is a journey filled with moments of joy and sorrow, achievements and challenges, expectations and disillusionments. There are times when we feel lost, uncertain of our direction and begin to question why we are walking a certain path. These are often signs that we are entering or are already in a state of personal crisis. Crises manifest in many ways such as emotionally, mentally, spiritually, and even physically. While emotional distress is often the most noticeable sign, the body also speaks through fatigue, restlessness, and illness. I would like to share some personal strategies that I have found useful not only for identifying when I'm in crisis, but for the purpose of discovering the deeper meaning behind it, and ultimately, reclaiming balance and alignment in life.

Suggested Steps to Find Your Purpose and Personal Balance

a) **Practice Self-Reflection:** Take time to explore your inner values and beliefs. Ask yourself what truly matters. Your core values serve as your personal compass, they help steer your decisions and actions. Reflect on goals you once held dear but may have abandoned due to life circumstances. Revisit them, redefine them, or set new ones. Make sure these goals are achievable and aligned with your sense of meaning, so that they motivate you rather than frustrate you.

b) **Seek New Experiences:** Engage in activities you've never tried before. Travel to unfamiliar places. Explore hobbies or pursuits that ignite your curiosity. Sometimes a fresh experience is enough to open the door to deeper insight and inspiration.

c) **Build Meaningful Connections:** Surround yourself with people who genuinely care about you, even if that means having only two or three close friends. Quality far outweighs quantity. Avoid relying on a large social circle that may disappear when you need them the most.

d) **Get Involved in Your Community:** It's human nature to feel joy when we give to others. Volunteering, mentoring, or simply offering support to those in need can be deeply fulfilling and restore a sense of purpose.

e) **Prioritize Self-Care:** Nobody can love or care for you better than yourself. Eat well, exercise, sleep adequately, read nourishing material, and honour your physical and emotional needs. These habits create a strong foundation for mental resilience.

f) **Engage in Prayer or Mindfulness Practice:** Connect with God, the Universe, or your higher self whatever resonates with you spiritually. Some call this mindfulness meditation, or simply soul-connection. It is a way to align your inner self with something greater, which brings peace and clarity.

g) **Seek Professional Support:** Mental health professionals can offer tools and techniques to help you process emotions and develop coping strategies. Support groups can also be powerful as they provide a safe space where shared experiences generate empathy, healing, and connection.

h) **Accept Your New Reality:** Flexibility is key to growth. Learn to accept change, acknowledge new circumstances, and look at them through a constructive lens. Every shift in life is an invitation to evolve.

i) **Cultivate Positivity and Gratitude:** If you constantly compare yourself to others or envy what they have, happiness will elude you no matter how well you fake it. Instead, focus on what you *do* have and appreciate it. Practicing gratitude uplifts your self-worth and fosters emotional healing.

j) **Give Without Expectation:** When you help others, do so with an open heart expecting nothing in return. Don't remind people of what you did for them, or boast about your generosity behind their backs. That attitude diminishes the value of your actions. You were placed in someone's life for a reason to offer support, love, and kindness. The Universe does not operate randomly; everything is intentional and connected. When balance is disturbed, life will find a way to restore it. Your role in others' lives is not about ego, but about purpose.

Transitioning Lives

While navigating the forest of crisis, you may feel both negative and positive emotions. The best way to move through the darkness is to raise your vibration, elevating your perspective and emotional state to a higher frequency. This doesn't mean ignoring pain; it means choosing to interpret your experiences through a more empowered, compassionate lens. Overcoming crisis is never easy. It demands perseverance, emotional resilience, inner strength, patience, and perhaps most importantly gratitude.

How to Be Grateful in Moments of Crisis (When It's Most Difficult)

Gratitude during a crisis may feel impossible, but it is one of the most powerful tools for transformation. To begin, remind yourself that everything you're experiencing has a purpose. You may not yet understand it, and the destination may be unclear, but the path was designed to make you stronger, more courageous, and more capable of entering the next phase of your life with greater awareness and inner depth. Crises are not just challenges; they are also invitations and opportunities. They offer you a choice to remain in the status quo, or to evolve into a more authentic, fulfilled version of yourself. Some crises arrive unexpectedly, while others are triggered by your own awakening, when something inside you finally decides that change is not only necessary but inevitable. If you ignore that call, your life may remain unchanged, but you risk facing regret for not acting when it mattered most.

Chapter 4: Life from Another Perspective

Opening the Mind to a Deeper Truth

Remove yourself just for a moment from the religious, cultural, or societal beliefs that have shaped your worldview since childhood. Give your mind the freedom to embrace new perspectives. What you were taught growing up is not necessarily the whole truth. Many people, at some point in life, ask: *Why do I exist? Why was I born into this particular family, with these parents, these challenges, and not others? Why do some people seem to have 'better luck' than me?* From a spiritual perspective, the answers to these questions are not rooted in coincidence or mere circumstance. According to spiritual teachings, as souls, we chose these very circumstances long before incarnating in this life. We selected our families, the challenges we would face, and even the pain we would endure all with the goal of accelerating our spiritual growth.

Incredible as it may seem, imagine for a moment that every relationship, every experience, and every challenge in your life has a deeper, higher purpose. This chapter invites you to explore that idea. It offers the possibility that souls after death actively choose their next earthly path, guided by divine wisdom and love. By opening your mind to this perspective, you may begin to understand your life differently, appreciate the relationships you've formed, and find purpose in the adversity you've experienced. If your heart and mind are ready to accept a deeper reality, then perhaps you can begin to view life not as a linear journey ending in physical death, but as a cycle of transformation, where death is simply the transition into another realm. In many spiritual traditions, this moment of death is described as a state of absolute clarity, the moment the soul detaches from the physical body and returns to its purest essence.

A Journey Back Home

Imagine death not as an ending, but as a return home; a realm where time and space no longer exist as we know them. In this realm, the soul enters a period of deep reflection, reviewing the events of its most recent life. This review is not about judgment, but about understanding what lessons were learned, which wounds remain, and what growth was achieved. From this sacred space, the soul begins preparing for its next reincarnation. This process is not done in isolation. The soul is lovingly guided by divine forces by God, the Universe, and a spiritual council made up of wise, benevolent beings. Together, they co-create guiding the soul's next journey. This includes choosing the major circumstances of the next life, selecting key individuals who will play important roles, and identifying life lessons that need to be addressed. While it may seem complex, this process has one primary objective: *to help the soul evolve, heal, and fulfil its spiritual mission.*

What Are We Learning Right Now?

Every person and situation in your life whether supportive or challenging is part of this divine plan. They reflect decisions your soul made before this incarnation, each one intended to teach you something essential. Everything begins with the soul's purpose. Each spirit has a unique learning path. Before reincarnating, it reviews unresolved lessons from previous lives and chooses a new life experience aligned with its growth goals. For instance, a soul may choose to be born into a family with financial hardship to learn resilience, perseverance, or the importance of gratitude. Another soul may choose loving, supportive parents to heal wounds from abandonment or rejection experienced in prior incarnations. Often, the people who challenge us the most are the ones helping us grow the most. These people may push us, inspire us, or test us urging us to expand beyond our perceived limits. I call them "Angels on Earth," as their presence reminds us that we are never truly alone. Have you ever felt an instant, inexplicable connection with someone? Or found that a particular relationship feels deeper than the rest? These souls or soulmates, are part of your spiritual family, connected to you in this life, in past lives, and likely in future ones. They leave lasting imprints on your soul.

The Reciprocity of Soul (Soulmates) Contracts

Most of these souls are not here just to support us, they also rely on us. Our destinies are often intertwined. We come together not only to help one another through life's trials but to collectively evolve toward a "higher soul's purpose." Through these relationships, we learn the value of empathy, sacrifice, and support. We begin to recognize karmic cycles unresolved patterns or relationships that we carry from one lifetime to the next. If past conflicts remain unresolved say, harm caused or forgiveness withheld, they become part of our karma, requiring eventual healing. For example, if someone harmed you in this life and you choose not to forgive, the karmic loop continues. Likewise, if you harmed someone and fail to seek forgiveness with a humble heart, you carry that burden into future incarnations.

But karma is not only about balancing wrongs. It is also about the gifts you bring into this life, gifts that bless others. Some people called this positive side *Dharma*. These include talents, leadership skills, creative energy, spiritual insight, or even profound empathy. Your mission might be artistic expression, healing, mentoring, or simply being a supportive presence for someone in need. These gifts are not random; they are echoes of your soul's accumulated wisdom reminders of the progress you have made in previous lifetimes. Some souls come equipped with deeper spiritual strengths, such as resilience, compassion, and forgiveness. And while life presents many obstacles, each one is a sacred mountain to climb, offering you a broader, more enlightened perspective.

Why Do Souls Reincarnate?

Why do souls return to this physical world again and again? The answer is rooted in the spiritual wish to contribute to universal balance and harmony. Even the souls that face the most painful circumstances, play a vital role in the divine design. The return to life is not a punishment it is an expression of love, a sacred choice made with the desire to grow, to serve, and to become closer to God. When you understand this, life ceases to feel like a series of random events. Instead, it reveals itself as a carefully crafted masterpiece. And when we eventually return to our Creator, we will uncover the most powerful truth of all, the master secret that links every experience, every soul, and every purpose.

The Master Secret: You Are Part of the Divine Design

Here is the truth: you, me, and every soul that has ever existed or will ever exist, is part of a divine plan that transcends our understanding. We are not here by accident. We are not powerless victims of fate. We are co-creators of our reality active participants in our soul's evolution. This divine plan is not rigid. It is fluid, responsive, and dynamic. But every thought, choice, and act of love we make, reverberates across the cosmos. Each decision, each moment of growth, adds to the harmony of what I call the *"Great Network of Energy"* or *"the Universe"* itself. By understanding this, you reclaim your power. You begin to see crisis as an opportunity, suffering as a teacher, and every life as a sacred mission. You are not merely surviving, you are evolving. You are not just living; you are fulfilling your divine purpose.

Chapter 5: The Final Stage of The Greater Plan

The Master Secret of the Universe

Finally, this greater plan of which we are all a part, assures us one fundamental truth: *We are never alone.* There are always spiritual souls guiding us, divine energies surrounding and supporting us on our journey. Every decision, every step forward, and every life lesson brings us closer to understand who we truly are. This is what I call *"the Master Secret of the*

Universe". The next time you face a challenge, an intense relationship, or a moment of deep uncertainty, remember this truth: **you are exactly where you need to be**, fulfilling a purpose that transcends what your eyes can see. Just like everyone else, *you are an irreplaceable part of this universal design*. Reaching this point of understanding is profound and it cannot be ignored.

I invite you now to pause and reflect on the important people in your life: your parents, your children, your friends, your partner and even those who have hurt you. What do you think they were meant to teach you? What aspect of your growth and evolution is connected to those relationships? Some answers may not be immediately clear. And that's okay. In time, life begins to reveal its hidden patterns, and what once felt confusing will start to make sense. Know this: you did not choose this life only for its moments of joy and triumph. You also chose the challenges, the heartbreaks, the tears, and the struggles because *you knew your soul would grow stronger, wiser, and more compassionate through them*. Even when the road feels uncertain or painful, every obstacle is crafted for your development. Each experience, whether uplifting or difficult, is designed to guide you closer to your divine essence.

The Sacred Opportunity to Evolve

The greatest gift you can give yourself is *to accept your life fully as it is,* with all its highs and lows. Not as a punishment. Not as random chance. But as a **sacred opportunity to evolve**.

When you begin to view your life this way, something remarkable happens. You move out of the role of victim and step into your true power as a **co-creator** of your own reality. You begin to live not from fear or resentment, but from a place of *gratitude and purpose*.

I invite you to look around your current environment with fresh eyes. Pay attention to the relationships you have, the challenges you're facing, the emotions rising within you. Ask yourself: **What is this teaching me today? How can I use this moment to grow?**

Even the experiences that seem small or insignificant carry meaning. Every moment in your life has a role to play. Every interaction is part of the divine orchestration of your soul's journey. When you begin to live with this awareness, you no longer chase purpose, you embody it. You realize that the journey itself *is* the purpose; and that through each trial, connection, and breakthrough, you are becoming who you were always meant to be.

Chapter 6: The New *"You"*

Free yourself from social expectations. The pressure to meet society's expectations can make you feel miserable and can affect your self-esteem. From a young age we are taught to adapt to society's expectations. We are told to dress in a certain way, act as expected, and even think the same as everyone else without autonomy. The pressure to meet these expectations can be overwhelming and make people feel like they are not living up to their full potential.

In this chapter, I will explore the different social expectations that individuals face, the impact these expectations can have on their lives, and how you can break the chains towards a *"New You"*.

What Are Some Chains That You Don't Even Perceive While Growing Up?

Gender expectations

One of the most prominent social expectations is gender expectations. From a young age, individuals are taught what is considered "masculine" or "feminine" behavior. Boys are told to be strong, aggressive, and not show their emotions, while girls are taught to be loving, emotional and submissive. These gender expectations can limit the expression of your true self and lead to feelings of confusion and frustration.

Professional expectations

Another social expectation that individuals face are professional expectations. Many people are pressured to pursue careers that are considered prestigious or that will bring them a high salary. This pressure can lead people to choose a career they are not passionate about, which can ultimately lead to dissatisfaction and unhappiness in their work.

Relationship expectations

Relationship expectations are also a common social expectation. People are often expected to marry, have children, and conform to traditional gender roles within their relationships. This pressure can lead people to enter into relationships that are not healthy or fulfilling for them.

Cultural expectations

Cultural expectations can also play an important role in the pressure to conform to social expectations. For example, in some cultures people are expected to care for their aging parents, even if it means sacrificing their own careers or personal lives. These cultural expectations can be difficult to navigate, especially for people trying to balance their cultural heritage with their own personal desires.

The impact of not meeting social expectations

When people do not meet society's expectations, they may face a variety of negative consequences. They may be excluded by their peers, families, friends, face discrimination in the workplace, or experience feelings of shame and inadequacy. These negative consequences can have a significant impact on an individual's mental health and well-being.

The pressure to meet society's expectations can be overwhelming and make people feel like they are not realizing their full potential. It is important for people to recognize these expectations and make a conscious effort to embrace their true selves, even if that means going against social norms. By doing so, people can live more authentic and fulfilling lives.

How to Find Real Freedom?

Social expectations can be a heavy burden that many people carry throughout their lives. The path towards freedom is finding your authenticity, accept your uniqueness, and find your own approach to this human life. How can we achieve this goal? I present some suggestions:

Embrace individuality and authenticity.

One of the first steps to freeing ourselves from social expectations is to accept our individuality and authenticity. Each person is unique, with their own set of talents, passions, and interests. By embracing our true selves and recognizing our passions, we can pave the way for personal growth and success, instead of conforming to societal norms. We should strive to create our own path and pursue what truly makes us happy.

Overcome fear and judgment.

Fear of being judged is a common barrier that prevents people from freeing themselves from social expectations. The fear of being seen as different or not fitting in, can be paralyzing. However, it is important to remember that true success and happiness can only be achieved by being true to yourself. Overcoming the fear of judgment requires courage and strong faith in yourself. It is essential to surround yourself with caring and understanding people who encourage you to achieve personal growth and self-expression.

Explore alternative paths.

To free ourselves from societal expectations, it is crucial to explore alternative paths that align with our passions and interests. This may involve taking risks and leaving our comfort zone. For example, instead of pursuing a traditional corporate career, one can choose to become an entrepreneur and follow their passion for a specific industry. Exploring alternative paths allows people to discover their true potential and create a fulfilling life on their own terms.

Challenge limiting beliefs.

Social expectations often arise from limiting beliefs that have been ingrained in us from a young age. These beliefs may include notions such as that success only comes from a certain career or that one must conform to traditional gender roles. Challenging these limiting beliefs is essential to freeing yourself from social expectations. By questioning and reevaluating these beliefs, people can open themselves to new possibilities and reconsider their own definitions of success and happiness.

The best option: authenticity and self-expression

After considering various perspectives and options, it becomes clear that the best way to free yourself from societal expectations is to embrace authenticity and self-expression. By staying true to ourselves and pursuing our passions, we can lead full and meaningful lives.

This may involve taking risks, challenging social norms, and stepping out of our comfort zones. However, the rewards of living authentically far, outweigh the temporary discomfort associated with freeing yourself from social expectations. Remember, you can live your life and accepting your true self. It is the key to achieve success on your own terms and evolve to a higher self.

Your life is like a flower, it needs water, nutrients, and care. If you silent your aspirations, your life becomes withered and your chances of achieving personal success are very slim.

Fear and insecurity are two of the most common emotions people experience. Avoid them because those emotions can lead to a lack of confidence, self-doubt, and a feeling of being trapped. However, it is possible to overcome these emotions and free yourself from social expectations using the following practices:

- *Recognize your fears and insecurities:* The first step to overcome fear and insecurity is to recognize them. This means recognizing when you are feeling fearful or insecure; identify the triggers that cause these emotions. Once you are aware of your fears and insecurities, you can start working to surpass them.

- *Challenging social expectations:* As mentioned before, society often sets expectations that are unrealistic or unattainable. It is important to challenge these expectations and question whether they are truly necessary or beneficial. Ask yourself if these expectations are aligned with your personal values and goals. If they don't, it may be time to let them go.

- *Focus on your strengths:* Instead of dwelling on your weaknesses and areas of insecurity, focus on your strengths. Identify your talents and abilities and find ways to use them to achieve your goals. This will help build your confidence and self-esteem, making it easier to overcome fear and insecurity.

- ***Surround yourself with people who support you:*** Having a support network of family and friends, can make all the difference in the world when it comes to overcoming fear, insecurity and challenges in general. Surround yourself with people who believe in you and encourage you to pursue your goals is essential for your growth.

- ***Practice self-care:*** Taking care of yourself is essential to overcome fear and insecurity. This includes getting enough sleep, eating well, exercising regularly, and doing activities that bring you joy and relaxation. When you take care of yourself, you are better equipped to face challenges and overcome fears.

- ***Seek help:*** If fear and insecurity are affecting your daily life, it may be time to seek professional help. A therapist or counselor can provide you with tools and strategies to overcome these emotions and free yourself from social expectations.

Overcoming fear and insecurity is a process that requires self-awareness, self-care, and a willingness to challenge society's expectations. By acknowledging your fears and insecurities, focusing on your strengths, surrounding yourself with supportive people, and seeking professional help, when necessary, you can free yourself from social expectations quicker and live a more authentic and fulfilling life.

- ***Free yourself from unrealistic expectations:*** One of the biggest obstacles to embrace authenticity, is the pressure to conform to unrealistic expectations. Whether it's from society, the media, family, or ourselves, we often feel the need to fit into a certain mold of how we should look, act, think, and feel. This can generate a lot of stress, dissatisfaction, and self-criticism. It can also prevent us from expressing our true selves and discovering our unique potential. In this final chapter, we are exploring how to free ourselves from unrealistic expectations and embrace our real bodies and selves without forgetting that all these efforts are part of the goal of true evolution.

We will now examine some of the sources and effects of these expectations, and some strategies for overcome them. Here are some of the points I would like to bring to your attention:

1. ***Common sources affecting our evolution:***
    - ❖ *Media and social networks.* We are constantly exposed to images and messages that portray idealized

standards of beauty, success, happiness, and lifestyle. These can create a false sense of what is normal, desirable and make us feel inadequate or inferior in comparison.

❖ *Family and friends.* Sometimes the people closest to us can also impose unrealistic expectations on us, whether intentionally or unintentionally. They may have certain beliefs, values, or preferences that they want us to follow or adopt, without considering our individuality or needs.

❖ *Ourselves.* We can also be our own worst critics and set unrealistic expectations for ourselves. We may have internalized the expectations of others or developed our own standards based on perfectionism, fear, or insecurity. We may judge ourselves harshly or punish ourselves for not meeting these expectations.

2. *Challenge unrealistic expectations. The next step is to question the validity and usefulness of these expectations. We can ask ourselves:*

❖ *Are these expectations realistic?* Many of the expectations we face are based on unrealistic or distorted assumptions, such as "I have to look like a supermodel to be attractive" or "I have to be successful at everything I do to be worthy." We can challenge these assumptions by seeking evidence that contradicts them or by considering alternative perspectives.

❖ *Are these expectations relevant?* Some of the expectations we face may not be relevant to our goals, values, or interests. For example, we may feel pressured to pursue a certain career path or lifestyle that does not align with our passions or purposes. We can challenge these expectations by clarifying what is important to us and what makes us happy and fulfilled.

❖ *Are these expectations useful?* Some of the expectations we face may not be helpful for our well-being, growth, or happiness. They can make us feel stressed, anxious, depressed, or frustrated. They can also limit our creativity, diversity, or authenticity. We can challenge these expectations by evaluating how they affect us and whether they serve or hinder us.

3. Replace unrealistic expectations with realistic ones. The last step is to replace unrealistic expectations with more realistic and positive ones. We can do this by:

❖ *Set "S.M.A.R.T." goals.* S.M.A.R.T. stands for Specific, Measurable, Attainable, Relevant and Time-bound. These are the criteria that can help us set realistic and meaningful goals that are aligned with our abilities, needs and aspirations. For example, instead of saying "I want to lose weight," we can say "I want to lose 5 kg in 3 months by following a healthy diet and exercise plan."

❖ *Focus on the process, not the result.* Instead of obsessing about the results or the end goal, we can focus on the journey and the progress we make along the way. We can celebrate our small victories, learn from our mistakes, and enjoy the experience. This can help us reduce stress, increase motivation, and improve performance.

❖ *Practice self-compassion.* Instead of judging ourselves harshly or comparing ourselves to others, we can treat ourselves with kindness, understanding, and acceptance. We can recognize our strengths, appreciate our efforts, and forgive our shortcomings. We can also remind ourselves that we are not alone and that we all struggle with unrealistic expectations at some point. This can help us increase our self-esteem, confidence, and happiness.

❖ *Educate and inspire others:* Educate others about the power of perception and the impact of social expectations on people's mental health and well-being, can be useful for your evolution and the ones who you share your experiences with. By sharing your own experiences and insights, you are inspiring others to evolve and see life different and we that can work collectively towards a more compassionate and caring society.

By freeing ourselves from unrealistic expectations, we can embrace our real bodies and live more authentically. We can express our true feelings, thoughts, and opinions, without fear of rejection or criticism. We can pursue our passions, interests, and dreams, without compromising our values or identity. We can also appreciate our uniqueness, diversity and potential, and contribute to the world in our own way. These practices will surely help us evolve, and when the time comes to reincarnate, we will be back with a higher perception of our true self and purpose.

Conclusion

In the end, what I have sought to share is simply a new perspective; one that invites us to reflect on the reasons *why* we are here in this life. I am fully aware that throughout the history of humanity, many thinkers, authors, and spiritual guides have attempted to answer these same questions. Some have done so through deeply traditional and conservative lenses, offering interpretations rooted in religious doctrine or philosophical systems that are very different from the approach I have chosen in this book.

Transitioning Lives

I do not claim to hold the absolute truth in what I have presented. Rather, I have offered a wider, more personal lens and a reflection based on what I have learned. I surely continue to learn, through my own experiences, challenges, and spiritual journey. This book is an honest attempt to share how I have come to perceive life at various points along my path, and how certain realizations have helped me make sense of both suffering and joy.

Ultimately, each of us must choose for ourselves. You have the power to accept, reject, or simply reconsider these ideas. You can take from them what resonates with you and leave aside what does not. The process of spiritual evolution is not a mandate; it is a personal calling. You may decide to embrace this broader perspective, or you may continue to live according to the beliefs instilled in you during childhood. Either way, the journey is yours.

What matters the most is for you to walk your path consciously, with an open heart, and with the courage to seek your own truth whatever form that may take.

About the Author

I am a soul, just like you, transitioning through this life with the goal of continuing our evolution towards our Creator. . . . . . .